Pigeon Point Lighthouse

View from the north, circa 1920. (Courtesy Rich Musante)

The
History
of

Pigeon
Point
Lighthouse

Frank Perry

GBH Publishing

Published by and available from:
GBH Publishing
Post Office Box 762
Soquel, California 95073

Manufactured in the United States of America

Library of Congress Catalog Card No. 86-82487
ISBN 0-943896-02-9

Also available by the same author:
Lighthouse Point: Reflections on Monterey Bay History
(History of the lighthouse at Santa Cruz, California)

Cover photo courtesy U.S. Coast Guard

for Jill and Sierra

Contents

Acknowledgments

It is a pleasure to acknowledge the many people who furnished information and photographs or in other ways helped with this book. I am indebted to the staffs of the following institutions and organizations for their help: The Bancroft Library, University of California, Berkeley; Society of California Pioneers Library; Map Library, Special Collections, and Government Publications sections of the McHenry Library, University of California, Santa Cruz; San Mateo County Historical Association Museum; Palo Alto City Library; Menlo Park Public Library; Redwood City Public Library; East Brother Light Station, Inc.; San Francisco Public Library; California Historical Society Library; Santa Cruz Public Library; National Archives, Washington, D.C.; Pigeon Point Hostel; National Maritime Museum, San Francisco; U.S. Lighthouse Society; and the Aids to Navigation Branch, Twelfth District, U.S. Coast Guard.

I would especially like to thank the following individuals: Gary Allen, Grace E. Baker, Rita Bottoms, Rev. and Mrs. Edward Conant, Steve Davenport, Ron Duarte and family, John Edmonds, Anne Goldberg, Nina Gordon, E. Colin MacKenzie, Rich Musante, Edith Perry, Jill Perry, Stan Stevens, and Wayne Wheeler. I am particularly grateful to Frank E. Davis and George and Jessie Davis for generously sharing with me their reminiscences and family photographs.

Finally, a special thanks to the Año Nuevo Interpretive Association and to the Sourisseau Academy for their grants aiding research and publication of this book.

Pigeon Point lighthouse. (Photo by the author)

Introduction

To most travelers along Highway 1 from San Francisco to Santa Cruz, Pigeon Point lighthouse is "that lighthouse down the coast." To mariners at night it is "flash white once every ten seconds." To sailors lost in the fog it is "dot, dash, dash, dot (pause) dot, dot"—the morse code signal sent forth by its radio beacon. To history buffs it is California State Historic Landmark Number 930.

Built in 1872, Pigeon Point lighthouse would easily qualify as a landmark, even if it were not officially so. And, like most stately old buildings, the lighthouse's history is embellished with a healthy share of rumors and legends. You need not travel far to learn something of its past. Many of the residents of neighboring farms and the small nearby town of Pescadero grew up in this region and speak affectionately of "their" lighthouse. Some relate the details of shipwrecks and other nineteenth century events almost as though they were first-hand accounts.

Standing at the base of the tower and gazing upward, it is easy to convince yourself that such a mighty and enduring structure must have been planned for this location from the beginning. It would seem to be the perfect lighthouse site: a bold, wind-swept promontory where ships still pass not too far offshore. In the mid-nineteenth century, however, government proposals for a lighthouse along this stretch of coastline focused at first on tiny Año Nuevo Island, six miles to the south. On clear days this island is plainly visible from Pigeon Point, low in profile, and separated from the mainland by a barely submerged rocky reef about a half mile wide. For nearly twenty years federal lighthouse authorities vacillated between building a lighthouse at Año Nuevo Island or one at Pigeon Point. Eventually, lights and fog signals were established at both locations.

Though the early histories of these two light stations are closely linked, the stations now stand in sharp contrast to one another. Abandoned in 1948, Año Nuevo Island lies deserted and dilapidated, its light tower collapsed, the station's days of glory and service to mariners having long past. Nature is slowly but surely reclaiming the island as wind and waves gnaw away at the remaining structures and sea lions and elephant seals take up residence in the abandoned keepers' house. At Pigeon Point, however, the pristine, white tower remains an active lighthouse. Automated in 1974, most of the station (excluding the light tower) was leased in 1980 to the State Department of Parks and Recreation. Today, in addition to being an aid to navigation, Pigeon Point light station also serves as a youth hostel.

Lighthouses were erected at over forty locations in California during the late 1800s and early 1900s. At some of these sites, several successive lighthouses were built. Sadly, only a few remain intact today. Some were lost through fires and earthquakes, others through demolition as the Coast Guard modernized and automated its facilities. Even Pigeon Point, which has one of the best preserved towers, looks quite different from the way it did in the 1870s. The original fog signal building was replaced by the present signal house in 1899. The water tanks which stood beside it are gone, as is the original two-story keepers' dwelling. I hope that this book, by chronicling the station's history, will give added meaning to the remaining historic buildings at Pigeon Point light station as well as encourage continued public support for their preservation.

The abandoned light station dwellings on Año Nuevo Island date from 1872 (left) and 1905. Photo taken in 1984. (Courtesy Steve Davenport)

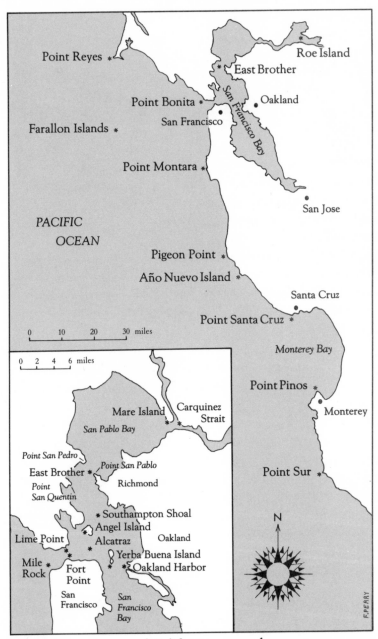

Lighthouses in central California, past and present.

A Shipwreck Legacy

No lighthouses were built in California under Spanish or Mexican rule, although this treacherous coast had claimed many vessels, including Spanish galleons. After the Mexican-American War, when California became part of the United States and the Gold Rush brought a flood of ships filled with hopeful miners and vital merchandise and supplies, the need for lighthouses became even more urgent. In response, Congress promptly funded plans for a chain of Pacific Coast beacons.

In 1849 a team of surveyors from the U.S. Coast Survey was dispatched to the West Coast to begin surveying the coastline and examining possible lighthouse sites. Based on these surveys and the recommendations of shipping concerns, sixteen lighthouses were erected along the West Coast during the 1850s. In California, lighthouses were constructed at Point Loma, Santa Barbara, Point Conception, Point Pinos, Humboldt Harbor, Crescent City, and at four locations to mark the entrance to San Francisco Bay: Point Bonita, Fort Point, Southeast Farallon Island, and Alcatraz Island. Six were built in what is now Oregon and Washington. When Congress approved these expenditures, apparently no one saw a need for a lighthouse at either Año Nuevo Island or what is now Pigeon Point, but that was soon to change. On June 6, 1853, the clipper ship *Carrier Pigeon* met her demise on the rocks at the point which still bears her name.

The decade of the 1850s could well be called the "Age of the Clipper." They were the sleekest and swiftest of merchant sailing vessels. The *Carrier Pigeon* measured 175 feet long and just 34 feet wide. She was rated at about 845 tons burden and boasted a beautiful gilded pigeon as a figurehead. Launched from the shipyards at Bath, Maine, in the fall of 1852, the *Carrier Pigeon* departed Boston on her maiden voyage January 28, 1853.

The ship took the waves with ease as she rounded Cape Horn and sailed north along the western edge of the Americas toward San Francisco. On the morning of June 6 she was sighted off Santa Cruz. The ship then continued northward as a thick fog blanketed the water, concealing the shoreline. By nightfall Captain Azariah Doane, believing he had veered far from shore, steered the vessel toward the coastline, hoping to catch sight of land. Suddenly, the sound of splintering timbers erupted as the ship's hull drifted into the grasp of the jagged sea bottom. Within fifteen minutes, seven feet of water was sloshing through the ship's hold. Fortunately, the captain and crew made it to shore safely, and the next morning they sent word of the disaster to San Francisco.

The news reached San Francisco the evening of June 7, and the U.S. Coast Survey steamer *Active* went to the scene to offer assistance. Soon, the sidewheel steamer *Sea Bird* also arrived, having been sent by the underwriters to salvage as much of the cargo as possible. The magnificent clipper was a sorry sight. Her hull was wedged firmly on a ledge of rocks just 500 feet from shore, the tide ebbing and flowing through the ship nearly up to her between decks.

The *Sea Bird* had been engaged in salvage work for only a day when it, too, ran into trouble. Early on the morning of June 10 heavy swells parted her bow anchor. Soon, her second anchor parted, and the jerking chain punctured her hull. Captain Wright got her under steam, but she was quickly taking on water. The captain had no choice but to beach her near Point Año Nuevo in hopes that she could eventually be repaired and refloated.

Now it was Captain Wright who was sending for help, which came this time from the steamer *Goliah*, also sent by the underwriters. The crew of the *Carrier Pigeon* and 1,200 packages of salvaged merchandise were safely transferred to the *Goliah* and taken to San Francisco. The *Goliah's* crew salvaged more cargo from the *Carrier Pigeon* over the next several weeks, but by the end of the month the clipper began breaking up. The *Sea Bird* was eventually refloated, but not until October.

The loss of the *Carrier Pigeon* was no small matter. The ship and cargo had been insured for about $195,000. Comparatively little of the cargo was recovered, and the ship, valued at $54,000, was sold as she lay for $1,500. News of the tragedy touched both coasts, and the location of the disaster would, from that time on, be called Pigeon Point.

The wreck was still fresh in the minds of the Coast Survey team when, in the fall of 1853, they began mapping the coastline between Santa Cruz and San Francisco. First they examined a site at Santa Cruz for which Congress had recently funded a lighthouse. They then traveled north and mapped Point Año Nuevo. The surveyors concurred that erection of a lighthouse at or near Año Nuevo was of greater importance. In a letter dated December 10, 1853, Lt. Comdg. T. H. Stevens wrote:

> In the first place, I consider it [Point Año Nuevo], from its character, an extremely dangerous point, and it should, therefore, have a light upon it for the purpose of warning the mariner of approaching danger. It possesses all the requisites, from its proximity to Santa Cruz, for a guide to that harbor; it would prove of advantage to vessels employed in the coasting trade; and, as it is frequently the first land made by vessels coming from distant ports, its importance is manifest in this connection. For these reasons, and from the fact that a lighthouse at Santa Cruz would only serve a local trade, I respectfully recommend the establishment of a light at Año Nuevo as of far greater importance.[1]

Stevens suggested that the lighthouse be built on the island, which at that time was connected to the mainland at low tide by a narrow sand spit. Coast Survey Assistant A. M. Harrison argued that the lighthouse should, instead, be established on Point Año Nuevo. Although the sector of visibility would be less, he said, the lighthouse would be more accessible, at a higher elevation, and on a more stable foundation. The recommendations of Stevens and Harrison were forwarded to the secretary of treasury, who was also ex officio president of the United States Lighthouse Board. In August, 1854, Congress appropriated additional funds, this time for a lighthouse at either Point Santa Cruz or Point Año Nuevo.

Not until 1855 was Pigeon Point first recommended as a lighthouse site. The previous December the surveyors mapped along the coast north of Point Año Nuevo and found Pigeon Point to possess "many advantages over Point Año Nuevo as a location for a lighthouse."[2] Coast Survey Assistant W. M. Johnson reported that this point was nearer to shipping lanes, had a boat landing that was protected from storms the majority of the year, and was composed of hard sandstone and conglomerate that would make for a better foundation than Año Nuevo point or island.

By 1857 lighthouse district inspector Hartman Bache, frustrated by delays in building a lighthouse at Point Santa Cruz, proceeded with plans for a Point Año Nuevo lighthouse. (In the late 1860s, the land title difficulties at Santa Cruz were finally resolved and a lighthouse erected there.) Major Bache still preferred Año Nuevo to Pigeon Point. A lighthouse was designed, and plans were drafted in keeping with the other sixteen lighthouses erected along the West Coast during this decade. It was to be a Cape Cod-style dwelling, made of brick and stone, with a tall, conical tower rising from it. The lantern room was to house a second-order fresnel lens with a focal plane about seventy-five feet above ground level. It would have most closely resembled the Cape Flattery lighthouse in Washington state, which was lighted in December of 1857 and still stands.

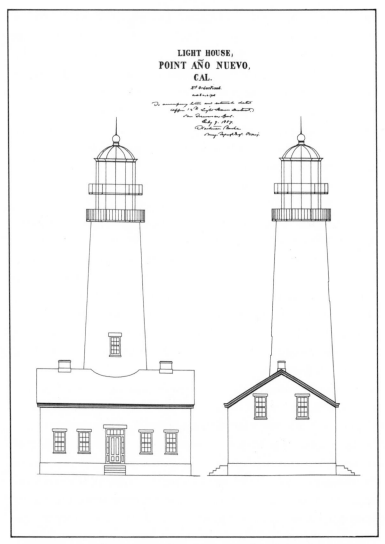

LIGHT HOUSE,
POINT AÑO NUEVO,
CAL.

Drawings made in 1857 for a proposed Point Año Nuevo lighthouse. The plans were never used. (Courtesy National Archives)

One can only speculate as to why these early lighthouse plans were not executed. In all likelihood, gaining proper title to the site was a problem here as at many proposed lighthouse sites in California. It is worth noting that the Rancho Punta del Año Nuevo land grant was not patented until December, 1857. Or perhaps construction was precluded by the political climate of the time and the impending Civil War. Only two more Pacific Coast lighthouses were completed by 1858. No others would be built until after the war.

During the 1860s three more ships met their fate along this stretch of coast, this time with terrible loss of life. Colonel Albert Evans painted a vivid description of the coast here in his 1889 book *A La California*. It is a place, he said, where "black reefs of rocks rear their ugly fangs, like wild beasts watching for their prey. A current sweeps in from Point Año Nuevo toward Pigeon Point, and many a vessel has been drawn in in the fog, to be dashed on the rocks." He further reported, "On the sandy bluff at Point Año Nuevo is an inclosure within which lie buried, side by side, forty of the victims of these terrible disasters."[3]

The first in this trilogy of tragedies was the *Sir John Franklin*. Like the *Carrier Pigeon,* it was an American clipper from the East Coast on its way to San Francisco. The date was January 17, 1865, and twenty-four hours had passed since the crew had sighted land through the thick fog. Captain John Despeaux, believing he was some sixty miles from shore, ordered a course change to the east. At nine o'clock that evening the crew suddenly found that the ship was in the breaker line. Before she could be directed away from shore, she struck bottom. Her timbers parted rapidly, splitting the ship in half and spilling her cargo and crew of twenty into the sea. Only eight made it to shore alive.

According to one account, a more complete wreck was seldom witnessed. The ship's entire cargo, including clothes, pianos, and whiskey, was "left to the mercy of the waves."[4]

The agent for the underwriters posted notice that any service rendered in saving goods from the vessel would be appropriately acknowledged. He warned, however, that anyone having property from the wreck who failed to give notice thereof would be prosecuted. As news of the wreck spread, however, people flocked to the scene like vultures and, according to the *San Mateo County Gazette,* many were "making a little" out of the misfortune.[5] Franklin Point, halfway between Pigeon Point and Point Año Nuevo, takes its name from the wreck.

Twenty-two months later came the loss of the British bark *Coya.* The *Coya* had departed Sydney, Australia, September 22, 1866, with a shipment of coal. In addition to her crew of twenty, ten passengers including several women and children were on board. After a brief stop at Pitcairn Island on October 13, she set sail for San Francisco. According to George Byrnes, one of the few survivors of the disaster, everything went well until November 24, "all of which day, and the day previous, we had very thick and squally weather."[6] Captain Paige and crew believed they were near the Farallones and, at about 7:30 P.M., were all down at tea. Suddenly the second mate reported land on the lee bow. Captain Paige immediately climbed on deck and ordered the ship turned around. As this was being done, she struck a reef. Mr. Byrnes wrote: "The sea kept lifting her from rock to rock, crushing her bottom in. She had at this time made considerably nearer land, and we all gave ourselves up for lost. The sea commenced breaking over the bow, carrying everything before it. . . . The scene now was something fearful; the main deck, being torn up by the pressure of water underneath, made one of the most frightful noises ever heard, the ladies screaming and being washed away one by one, and drowning under the lee rigging."[7] The ship, cargo, and twenty-six lives were lost.

Both shipwrecks drew nationwide attention, including that of government lighthouse authorities. They responded quickly. According to maps in the General Land Office, it appeared

Old photograph of grave marker which stood for many years at Franklin Point. It said, "To the Memory of Edward J. Church of Baltimore, Md., Aged 16 years, And the Ten other Seamen lost on Ship Sir John Franklin, January 17, 1865." (Courtesy Edward Conant)

that Año Nuevo Island was not included in the patent for the Año Nuevo rancho. Since the island was supposedly unclaimed, President Andrew Johnson declared it a government reservation for lighthouse purposes. Due in part to the efforts of U.S. Senator Cornelius Cole, Congress on July 20, 1868, appropriated $90,000 for establishment of a first-order lighthouse at "Point Año Nuevo or vicinity." Plans for a lighthouse were again underway, but not soon enough to prevent still another wreck—that of the *Hellespont* in November, 1868.

The circumstances surrounding the loss of the *Hellespont* were frighteningly similar to those of the *Coya*. Like the *Coya*, she was sailing from Australia to San Francisco with a load of coal. For three days before to the disaster, there had been thick clouds with light mist, later turning into rain. Due to the overcast sky, Captain Soule had been unable to make reliable astronomical observations to determine his position. On Wednesday, November 18, the captain ordered the ship more to the northeast and guessed that they would sight land by daybreak. At twenty minutes before five the following morning, seaman Charles Wilson, the lookout, shouted "breakers ahead." All hands leaped out of their bunks, sprang on deck, and attempted to turn the ship away. Their efforts proved to be in vain as heavy rollers began pounding against the side of the vessel. Just ten minutes after the breakers were first sighted, the ship struck the bottom. The first strike was light, but then an extraordinarily large wave lifted the ship up and brought her down with such tremendous force that she was smashed to pieces.

The crew clung fearfully to the bits of floating wreckage, struggling through the darkness toward shore. Remarked one of the crew, "Captain, you were a little nearer to shore than you thought you were."[8] Just seven of the eighteen-man crew survived.

Erecting the Light

As news of the *Hellespont* disaster spread, public outcry over lack of a lighthouse grew quickly. On November 28, 1868, H. A. Scofield, editor of the *San Mateo County Gazette,* eloquently summarized the urgent need for a lighthouse:

The recent terrible wreck of the ship *Hellespont* at Pigeon Point in this county, which resulted in the loss of eleven of her crew, including Captain Soule, constitutes another appeal to the government at Washington for the establishment of a lighthouse at Pigeon Point. Several vessels have been wrecked in that vicinity within the past few years, in every instance of which, many lives have been lost, and the vessels invariably a total loss. Pigeon Point is the most extensive promontory on the coast south of the Golden Gate, and which point seems especially adapted for a light-house. No other one place on the Pacific Coast has proved so fatal to navigators as this locality, and it behooves those most interested in maritime affairs on the coast as well as in the East to bring their influence to bear immediately upon the government officials, and never relax their efforts until a light-house is erected at Pigeon Point. . . . If we are not mistaken, it is a matter of fact that all of the vessels that have been lost in the vicinity of Pigeon Point have been wrecked in consequence of dense fogs which prevented the land from being sighted until the vessels were among the breakers. A fog-bell or whistle would unquestionably in most instances be found more useful than a light. Either a bell or whistle of sufficient volume at Pigeon Point would have saved the *Hellespont,* the *Franklin* and other vessels which have been lost in that vicinity. Our delegates in Congress are expected to make it their business to look after this matter, and they should not be permitted to forget the interests of their constituents.

One of San Francisco's papers, the *Daily Alta California,* castigated the Lighthouse Board and the district engineer for the delays in lighthouse construction. "The public of California have been waiting for eighteen years to have their Government provide *one* light-house for the ninety miles of coast lying south of the Golden Gate," it said. "There has never been a light there and, from present appearences, there never will be." The newspaper continued its indictment:

> Sixteen years ago Professor Bache made most elaborate and voluminous reports upon the fitness of these two points for light-house sites, all of which were nicely printed and illustrated and bound up and paid for, and then packed away in the Congressional Library. The volumes are covered with dust; the Professor himself has died and gone to join the shades of those wrecked mariners whose sad fate would have been avoided had his teachings been heeded; and still the light-house at New Year's Point [Año Nuevo] is only a thing talked about.
>
> Will it be said that Senator Cole got a Congressional appropriation of $90,000 last spring to build a light-house at New Year's Point? And will men suppose that therefore there is to be a light there? Nay, nay. There shall be more inquiries, more reports, more paper, more ink, more tape, but no more light.[9]

Lt. Col. Robert S. Williamson, an army engineer on detached duty with the lighthouse service, was charged with supervising construction of lighthouses in California at that time. Williamson said he had not yet received instructions from Washington, D.C., stemming from the Congressional appropriation. To make matters worse, Año Nuevo Island, which had supposedly been reserved by the president for a lighthouse, was being claimed by the owners of Año Nuevo Rancho. Further investigation proved the owners' claim to be valid, thus necessitating purchase of the island by the government before a lighthouse could be erected.

Loren Coburn and his brother-in-law, Jeremiah Clarke, had purchased the 17,000-acre rancho in 1862 for about $30,000.

Clarke was an attorney, while Coburn had made his money during the Gold Rush. Coburn was said to have been rather shy and inoffensive in manner by those who met him, but this was a deceptive exterior. He was a shrewd, unscrupulous business-man whom many people disliked. Even before Coburn and Clark had purchased the rancho, they had made arrangements to lease much of the land at a handsome profit to a group of dairymen: Horace Gushee, Charles H. Willson, R. E. Steele, I. C. Steele, and E. W. Steele. The two men knew about the lighthouse proposals and surveys of the 1850s and, realizing the chance to sell the sites to the government at great profit, purposely excluded Año Nuevo Island and Pigeon Point from the land they leased.

Coburn and Clarke reportedly demanded $40,000 for the island alone—more than they had paid for the entire rancho. Lt. Col. Williamson, acting on behalf of the Lighthouse Board, offered $5,000. The government then raised its offer to $10,000, but Coburn and Clarke would not budge. There was little progress in negotiations until April, 1870, when the govern-ment threatened to condemn the land. Finally, on May 18, 1870, the deed was signed. The government purchased a total of nineteen and a half acres: one and a half acres at the tip of Pigeon Point, a nine-acre tract located about 500 yards inland from the point for "water privileges," and the nine-acre Año Nuevo Island.

The negotiations had taken so long that most of the light-house appropriation (except for the amount spent to purchase the land) reverted to the U.S. Treasury. Not until March 3, 1871, did Congress reappropriate the funds—another $90,000.

As late as December, 1870, there had still been discussion as to whether Año Nuevo Island or Pigeon Point would be the best site for a lighthouse. By the following spring, however, it was decided to erect a first-order lighthouse and fog signal at Pigeon Point and to establish only a fog signal at Año Nuevo. Año Nuevo Island fog signal station began operation May 29,

Phineas F. Marston. (From *History of Alameda County* published by M.W. Wood, 1883)

1872. It was manned by the Lighthouse Service, as were light stations, even though a light was not added until the 1890s.

Construction at Pigeon Point commenced soon after the 1871 appropriation. In charge of the operation was Phineas F. Marston, who had begun his career as a New England carpenter and builder of churches and army barracks. In 1858, at age forty-five, he came to San Francisco with his wife and family and was placed in charge of construction of the barracks at the Presidio, Black Point (Fort Mason), and Angel Island. His fine work attracted the attention of Lt. Col. Williamson, who subsequently hired him to build several West Coast lighthouses. Marston's first job with the Lighthouse Service was construction of the Ediz Hook lighthouse along the Strait of Juan de Fuca in what is now Washington state. This was followed by other Washington lighthouses and, in 1870, the lighthouse and fog signal building at Point Reyes. He would go on to build the stations at Año Nuevo Island and Point Montara as well.

By June, 1871, Marston and his crew were at work on the Pigeon Point tower, dwelling, and fog signal building. The latter were to be simple wooden structures, but erection of the tower would be more of a challenge and would be further supervised by a Mr. Wallace. The floor at the base of the tower was to be over 8 feet thick, the walls 4½ feet thick. When completed, the focal plane of the lens would be 100 feet above ground level, or about 150 feet above the sea. It is today tied with Point Arena as the tallest active lighthouse on the West Coast. Because high cliffs border much of the western shore, tall light towers, so common on the East Coast, were seldom needed here.

The government often used one set of plans for several lighthouses, varying them only slightly. Such was the case with Pigeon Point. Indeed, on the original plans the name "Pigeon Point" was pasted over that of another lighthouse. Pigeon Point bears a striking resemblence to Bodie Island and Currituck Beach lighthouses in North Carolina, Charleston lighthouse in South Carolina, and Yaquina Head in Oregon. All differ in height but are otherwise virtually identical in appearance.

Materials for the light station came from many different sources, some nearby, some far away. Lumber was purchased from the firm of Chandler and Harrington, proprietors of Glen Mills along nearby Whitehouse Creek. The stairs, platforms, balcony, and other iron work were fabricated by Nutting & Son, San Francisco. The lens was manufactured by the firm of Henry-Lepaute in Paris, France. The lantern room was constructed at the Lighthouse Service general depot in New York.

Perhaps most important are the estimated 500,000 bricks used to build the tower. A visitor to Pigeon Point in early June, 1871, announced, "Men are already at work making the brick on the government ground some forty or fifty rods back from the site selected for the erection of the light-house."[10] Apparently, this brick was of unsatisfactory quality. A memorandum concerning Pigeon Point written to Assistant Lighthouse Engineer Eusebio J. Molera stated: "No brick except city brick

Keepers' dwelling shortly after completion. Photo by Eadweard Muybridge. (Courtesy The Bancroft Library)

to be used in completing the tower. The brick hauled from the kiln of brick on the 9 acre lot to be hauled back there *without expense to the U.S.* If any of those bricks have been put in the tower they must be taken out and hauled back to the kiln."[11] According to still another account, the bricks were made in Pescadero. In any event, they came from a fairly local source. They were certainly not brought "around the Horn from

Norfolk, Virginia," as has frequently been written. Even for the earliest lighthouses built in California, local sources were tapped for brick and stone.

The trouble with the bricks noted in the memorandum was but one of many delays in construction. On September 10, 1871, the fog signal went into operation under the command of keeper J. W. Patterson and one assistant. The tower, however, still stood uncompleted. That winter, torrential rains further slowed the operation. By the following March, the spiral staircase was being installed, but the workman had difficulty determining where all the pieces went. In addition, it seemed that some pieces were missing. At the request of Molera, the machinist who had assembled the staircase in Mr. Nutting's shop was sent to the lighthouse to show the men how the pieces fit together. In April work ceased, awaiting arrival of the lantern room, at that time expected to be shipped from New York around May 1. On July 6, 1872, the *San Mateo County Gazette* reported, "The light, first-class, is on the ground, but not yet up, the workmen having suspended their labors some time ago for reasons known only to the Government."

Not until November did Captain Charles J. McDougal, the lighthouse inspector, formally examine the station and pronounce it ready for lighting. Thomas J. Winship, the district lampist, readied the oil lamp and instructed the keepers on the particulars of its use. At sunset on Friday, November 15, 1872, the brass clockwork began ticking, the smell of burning lard oil filled the lantern room, and the powerful beacon cast its first rays across the Pacific.

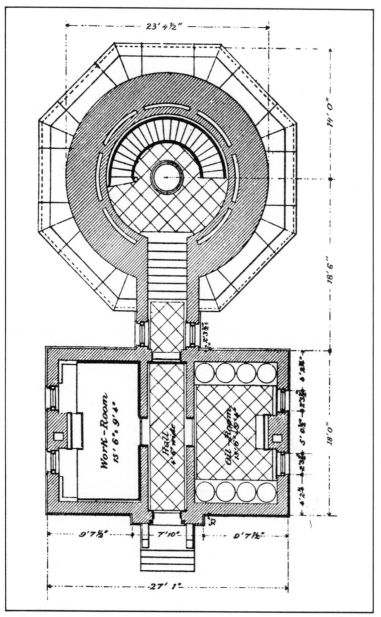

Floor plan for the tower showing location of oil and work rooms. (Courtesy National Archives)

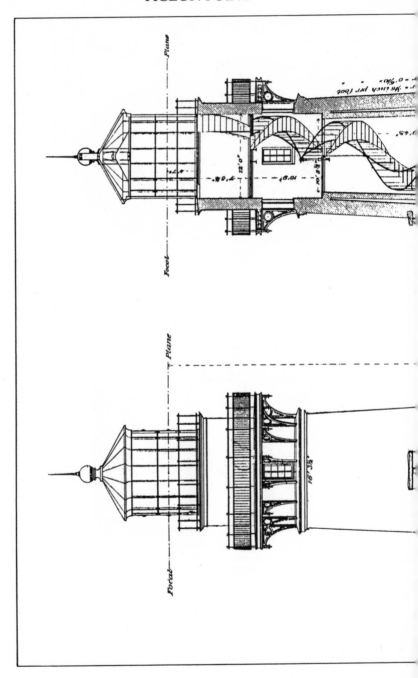

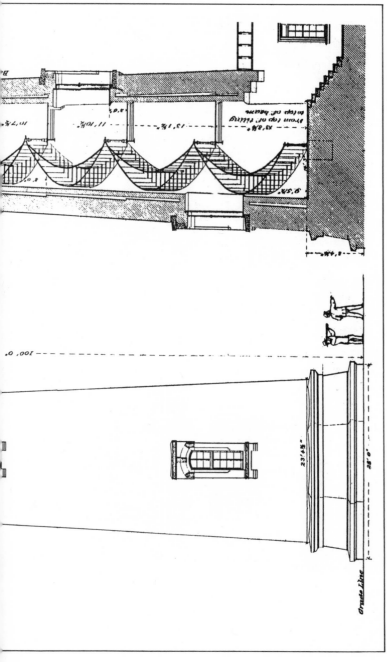

One of the original drawings used in constructing the lighthouse. (Courtesy National Archives)

Base of lens. (Photo by the author)

Lamps, Lenses, and Illuminants

Pigeon Point light station was built to serve several purposes: as a warning of danger, as a guide for coastal vessels, as a landfall for ships arriving from across the ocean, and as a day mark. Being a major seacoast light, Pigeon Point was equipped with a first-order lens, the largest and most powerful lens used in lighthouses on the Pacific Coast of the United States. Of the over forty lighthouses eventually built in California, most of those on the outer coast utilized lenses of this size. In northern California these included Point Sur, Southeast Farallon Island, Point Reyes, Point Arena, Cape Mendocino, and St. George Reef.

The great Scottish lighthouse engineer, Alan Stevenson, once remarked, "Nothing can be more beautiful than an entire apparatus for a fixed light of the first order. . . . I know of no work of art more beautiful or creditable to the boldness, ardor, intelligence, and zeal of the artist."[12] Having devoted his life to lighthouses, Stevenson was of course biased, but anyone who has seen a first-order lens is sure to agree that it is not only a remarkable engineering feat but also a work of art. Pigeon Point's lens comprises 1,008 separate lenses and prisms, each ground and polished by hand to exacting specifications and meticulously mounted in a brass framework. Six feet in diameter and seventeen feet high, the entire apparatus weighs over four tons. It focused the light from an oil lamp and later an electric light bulb mounted inside at the focal plane. The light from the lamp or bulb, which radiated out in all directions, was reflected and refracted by the lenses and prisms so as to be cast seaward. The lens made efficient use of about 80 percent of the light.

This type of lens is called a fresnel lens (pronounced fray-*nell*), named for French physicist Augustine Jean Fresnel, who perfected it in 1822. Fresnel had been commissioned by the French government to develop a better lighting system for that nation's lighthouses. Rather than trying to devise a brighter light source, Fresnel concentrated his research on making more effective use of the light. At that time parabolic reflectors, shaped from metal and silvered, were placed behind lamps to focus the light seaward. These did not work well, however, and Fresnel decided to try using glass lenses to focus the light. It would have been impractical to mold a single piece of glass into a lens large enough for lighthouse use, so he conceived the idea of using many small lenses and prisms arranged in a stair-step fashion. It was one of those great moments in the history of technology when everything falls into place and a multitude of problems are solved simultaneously. The new lenses focused the light very precisely, could be disassembled and shipped in sections, and could be used to produce a virtually limitless number of light characteristics.

Fixed lenses spread the light evenly in all directions and thus showed a continuous light. Rotating lenses, like Pigeon Point's, produced flashing lights. These lenses separated the light into individual beams, each radiating outward like the spokes of a wheel. The lenses were mounted on wheels and rotated very slowly by means of a clockwork mechanism. As the lens turned, mariners would see a flash of light every time a beam was cast in their direction.

The Pigeon Point lens has twenty-four flash panels, each of which produced a beam of light. When the keeper wound up the weight and engaged the clockwork, the lens completed one rotation every four minutes. Since one twenty-fourth of four minutes is ten seconds, Pigeon Point's flash pattern was one flash every ten seconds.

Mariners could distinguish between lighthouses by their differing characteristics. In 1890, for example, Santa Cruz had a fixed red light; Southeast Farallon Island produced a white flash once each minute; Point Bonita had a fixed white light; Point Reyes showed a white flash once every five seconds. In all, some seventeen different light characteristics were used at that time. Lighthouses are still distinguished in this way, but most have different characteristics than in the old days. Pigeon Point is unusual in that its signal has remained unchanged throughout its long history.

No one knows exactly how much the government paid for Pigeon Point's lens. Arnold Johnson, in his 1890 book *The Modern Lighthouse Service,* lists first-order lenses as costing between $4,250 and $8,400. Today, they are considered priceless.

No other aspect of this lighthouse's past has attracted such wide attention as the mysterious early history of its lens. A brass plate attached to the lens base gives the name of the manufacturer as Henry-Lepaute. This firm was one of three Paris optical companies that produced lighthouse lenses. The other two were Sautter, Lemonnier & Cie, and Barbier & Fenestra. The United States bought nearly all of its fresnel lenses from France, as did most of the rest of the world.

After the lens was shipped to the United States, the mystery begins. According to Edward Rowe Snow in his *Famous Lighthouses of America* (1955), the lens was previously used at "Fort Sumter Light, Charleston, South Carolina, where it had been buried on Charleston beach to prevent its destruction during the war between the North and the South." A 1939 WPA guidebook, *California: A Guide to the Golden State,* reported, "The powerful lens was used first on the New England and later on the South Atlantic coast where it was buried in the sand during the Civil War, according to one story, to keep it from falling into Confederate hands." An article in the *San Francisco Call* dated May 24, 1896, stated that the lens was

Brass plate attached to the base of the lens. (Photo by the author)

supposedly first used at Cape Hatteras, North Carolina. It also reported that the lens was buried in the sand during the Civil War, and that some of the rebels must have dug it up since it was next found "in an old warehouse in New Orleans about 1868." In 1883 one of the keepers said in an interview that the lens was captured by the Confederates while being imported from France but was later recaptured by the Federals. "This fact," he told the reporter, "will shine in future history."[13]

One of the earliest versions of the story appears in the *Illustrated History of San Mateo County, California,* published only six years after the lighthouse began operation:

> The lens of the Light House has also a historic interest, having formerly been in use on the Atlantic Coast at Cape Hatteras, where it was captured by the Confederates during the War of the Rebellion and afterwards recaptured by Federal forces. The present management of the Government Works here is under the charge of a faithful and gallant ex-soldier of the Union Army, Mr. C. H. Howard.[14]

An article published in the *San Mateo County Gazette* at the time the lighthouse was first lighted corroborates the story that the lens was used previously at Cape Hatteras. The stories of the lens being captured during the Civil War, however, are doubtful. The most definitive statement on the matter comes from Commissioner of Lighthouses George R. Putnam in a letter dated May 2, 1924. Putnam, who was in charge of the nation's lighthouse system at that time, was also a historian. In response to an inquiry about the lens's history by the district superintendent, Harry Rhodes, Putnam wrote:

> You are advised that the lens now at Pigeon Point appears to be the *second* lens placed in commission at Cape Hatteras Light Station, North Carolina, in 1863, following what is said to have been the destruction of the lantern and original lens placed at this station in 1854. There is also a notation on the records here that the *original* lens was carried by Confederate agents to Raleigh and was subsequently recovered, but it is difficult to state whether these statements are true or not for the files of the Bureau covering this period were badly burned a few years ago and are difficult of access.
>
> However, the second lens, the one now in commission at Pigeon Point, was discontinued in 1870 when the new (present) tower at Cape Hatteras was established, and there is a record here that it was placed in storage at the General Lighthouse Depot on January 17, 1871, and on August 11, 1871, was shipped to Pigeon Point.[15]

The light source, too, has fallen victim to historical romanticism. It has often been written that Pigeon Point lighthouse originally used a whale oil lamp. Some of California's earlier lighthouses relied on sperm whale oil, but by the late 1860s these and other United States lighthouses had been converted to lard oil. The reason for the switch was simple economics. During the mid 1800s the price of sperm oil continued to rise as sperm whale populations declined and the industrial demand for the oil increased. Experiments by Professor Joseph Henry, member of the Lighthouse Board and secretary of the Smithsonian Institution, revealed that lard oil would work just as well and at about half the price.

The claim that Pigeon Point used (or was to use) whale oil

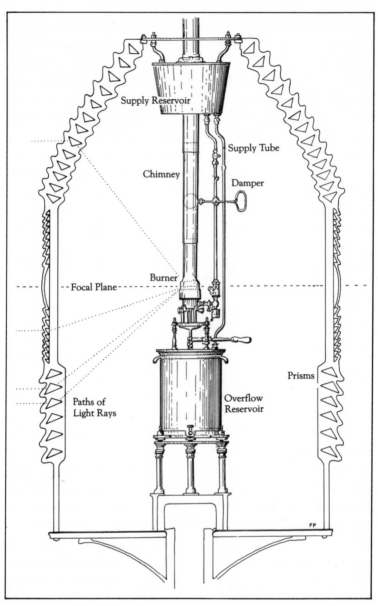

Cross section of lens showing lard oil lamp and paths of light rays. (Drawing by the author)

began even before the light was first lighted. In May of 1872 Capt. Patterson, the keeper, said to an interviewer that as soon as the nearby Portuguese whalers could catch and try out a whale, the lamp would be filled, installed, and set "exchanging winks and blinks with its neighbor of the Farallones on moonlight nights."[16] This was the same keeper who claimed that the fog signal was produced by two large bulls hung up by their tails alternately every seven and forty-five seconds.

The lard oil lamp used at Pigeon Point stood eight feet high and was made of brass with a slender, glass chimney. The main reservoir for the oil was a doughnut-shaped container near the top of the lamp, encircling the chimney. The heat from the flame below kept the oil liquid in cold weather. Fumes from the lamp escaped through the ventilator ball on the lantern room roof.

Around 1888 Pigeon Point's lard oil lamp was replaced by one that burned kerosene. New containers were also supplied to the station to store the more volatile and dangerous fuel. Kerosene was an even cheaper fuel and, by 1890, had entirely replaced lard oil in United States lighthouses. In the early 1900s a separate oil house was constructed away from the tower to prevent damage to the lighthouse in event of fire or explosion. Before this, the oil was stored in the oil room at the base of the tower.

Both the lard oil and kerosene lamps were wick lamps. The kerosene lamp, called a Funk's Mineral Oil Lamp, had five wicks arranged concentrically. Each day the keepers had to trim the wicks as part of their duties.

During fiscal year 1911-12 the kerosene wick lamp was replaced by an incandescent oil vapor lamp (abbreviated I.O.V.). The device worked similarly to the Coleman lamps used today by campers. Kerosene was forced under pressure into a vapor chamber where it was converted to a gas. Then it passed through small holes upward to the mantle, where the gas was ignited to produce a brilliant white light. The I.O.V.

A young lighthouse visitor gazes through the lens. (Photo by the author)

lamp was a great improvement over the kerosene wick lamp, producing a brighter light with no increase in fuel consumption. In 1912 Pigeon Point was rated at 160,000 candlepower with a visibility of eighteen miles.

Conversion to electricity occurred around 1926. The one thousand watt light bulb boosted the station's output to 680,000 candlepower and relieved keepers of many of their chores. The electric light did not smoke up the glass or require the degree of maintenance and supervision of the earlier lamps. In fact, Pigeon Point was converted from a four-man station to a three-man station soon after electrification.

The Fog Signal

Even powerful lights like Pigeon Point's can be rendered useless in thick fog or rain. Despite this, fog signals were not put into common use at United States lighthouses until the mid-1800s. Though people often speak of fog "horns," a bewildering assortment of noise-making devices has been used through the years to guide mariners, including cannons, bells, gongs, trumpets, whistles, and sirens. In 1869 steam whistles, similar to those on locomotives and ships, were put into regular operation at two lighthouses in Maine. These proved to be quite practical to operate and were the most powerful fog signals devised up to that time. Steam whistles were soon installed at many coastal locations, including Pigeon Point and Año Nuevo Island. By June, 1873, five such devices were in use in California, with three more planned.

The Pigeon Point fog signal building housed one, and later two, steam plants, each connected to a whistle mounted on the roof of the building. (The second was added as a back-up system.) Each steam plant consisted of a firebox, a boiler, a smokestack, and a timing device to regulate whistle blasts. Cordwood from nearby mills was purchased for fuel, and water for the boilers was piped from a well on the nine-acre plot north of the lighthouse.

Fog signals were assigned different characteristics so that mariners could distinguish one station from another. Pigeon Point's whistle blasts were four seconds in duration, separated alternately by seven and forty-five seconds of silence. In contrast, the signal at Año Nuevo Island produced ten-second

Original fog signal building, 1870s. (Courtesy The Bancroft Library)

blasts at intervals of fifty-five seconds.

Contemporary accounts frequently compared the sound of the signal with that of cows. One visitor reported that it resembled an "asthmatical old bovine," and claimed that had it been located closer to Pescadero, residents there would have been entitled to damages sufficient to bankrupt the government.[17] Another said it sounded like a "stuck hog," or, at a distance, "a cow in distress."[18] The first night that one of the local dairymen, William Pinckham, heard the signal, he indeed mistook it for a cow in distress and believed that a grizzly bear was preying upon his stock. He rounded up five or six armed men, and they crept out into the darkened pasture. Of course, no bear was found. Not until the following morning did they learn the embarrassing truth about the origin of the noise. Another story in a similar vein was told by the residents of the Steele Ranch near Año Nuevo Island. When the whistle on the island sounded for the first time, nearby cows stampeded across the fields down to the beach. Mrs. Steele exclaimed that they must have thought there was a wonderful bull down there!

The signal, though it could usually be heard for several miles, was not without its problems. The sound resembled a ship's whistle, and thus there was the danger of confusing mariners. Another disadvantage was that the boiler took forty-five minutes to develop sufficient steam pressure. To minimize delays, wood was placed in the firebox and readied for lighting at a moment's notice. As at most stations, Pigeon Point also had water problems. The well water was found to contain minerals destructive to boiler tubes. In the early 1880s, a 20,000-square-foot rainshed was laid on the nine-acre lot, and two storage tanks for the captured water were erected beside the signal house. Even so, the equipment needed regular repairs and replacement parts. In 1899 the entire signal house was replaced by the fog signal building that stands today.

The whistle operated an average of 900 hours per year and consumed about 1 cord of wood for every 10 hours of use. In 1897, for example, the signal operated a total of 739 hours and consumed about 69 cords of wood. On one occasion, the signal ran night and day for six weeks. Foggier stations, such as Point Bonita, forty miles to the north, frequently blasted away for well over 1,000 hours per year. During one year, a lightship anchored off the coast of San Francisco logged 2,221 hours of fog—over three months' worth.

In 1911 the whistle was replaced by a first-class compressed-air fog siren. Its sound was produced by a revolving cylinder or disk with slots in it. Air forced through the slots vibrated to produce the note, which was amplified by an attached horn. The air compressor was powered by a gasoline engine, enabling operating pressure to be attained in just a few minutes. The siren had a different characteristic from the whistle: two-second blasts alternately separated by six seconds and twenty seconds of silence.

In 1935 the siren was superseded by a two-tone diaphone. It is the mournful "bee-ohh" of the diaphone that people most often associate with foggy coastlines. A Canadian invention, the diaphone was first introduced in the United States in 1915. By the 1930s it had come into common use in this country. Like the siren, it ran on compressed air. At Pigeon Point the siren's characteristic was adopted for the diaphone as well, and the siren was maintained for many years as a back-up signal.

Compressed air for the diaphone was pumped into giant steel tanks and maintained at about forty pounds pressure. A slotted reciprocating piston produced the two-tone sound, which had a normal range of four to five miles. The diaphone remained in use at Pigeon Point until the mid 1960s. Three of the large air tanks can still be seen inside the signal house.

The diaphone was even more powerful than the siren, but it required large quantities of compressed air. It was replaced in the mid-1960s by the smaller and more efficient diaphragm. It was mounted on the side of the lighthouse tower in front of the lower window. The single-note sound was produced by a vibrating metal diaphragm regulated by a series of valves that produced differential air pressure.

Earlier, before the diaphragm replaced the diaphone, another important navigational aid was added to the station. In 1943 a tall antenna was installed that beamed forth a morse code radio signal unique to Pigeon Point. A real technological breakthrough, the radio beacon could be detected 100 miles away. By means of radio direction finders in combination with other radio beacons along the coast, mariners could determine their position through triangulation, no matter what the weather. In later years, the radio beacon was synchronized with the diaphone for distance finding. Since both "sounded off" simultaneously, the mariner could calculate his approximate distance from the point by counting the number of seconds between picking up the radio signal in his receiver and

Radio beacon controls in the fog signal building, 1950. (Courtesy U.S. Coast Guard)

hearing the diaphone.

In recent years, radar, radio direction finders, and loran receivers have become standard equipment even on small vessels. This led to the discontinuation of the audible fog signal at Pigeon Point in 1976. Though the radio beacon is still in use, it is likewise gradually becoming outmoded as many mariners rely increasingly on loran and as larger vessels turn to satellite navigation.

Pigeon Point light station, 1890s. (Courtesy San Mateo County Historical Museum)

Life at Pigeon Point

In the lonely watches of the dreary, stormy night, with the fury of the wind about him, and with the roar of the breakers dashing against the rocks below him, . . . sits the keeper, true to his trust, faithful to his charge, doing well and honestly his duty, keeping his lamp trimmed and burning, sending forth the ray to guide and make glad the storm-encircled sailor.

History of San Mateo County, California, 1883

Over a dozen men served as principal keeper at Pigeon Point between 1871 and 1939. Dozens more served there through the years as assistant keepers, residing at the station with their families. From 1939 to 1981 coastguardsmen carried on the lightkeeping tradition.

From 1852 until 1910, America's lighthouses were administered by a nine-member board composed of army and navy officers and civilian scientists—all appointed by the president. The Lighthouse Board did much to improve the quality of aids to navigation in this country as well as the caliber of Lighthouse Service personnel. Although the Lighthouse Service was a civilian organization, it had a distinct military flavor during this period. Each district had a naval officer in charge of personnel and an army engineer to oversee lighthouse construction and repairs. The naval officer, as district inspector, regularly examined each light station and delivered keepers their pay.

Many of Pigeon Point's keepers had had previous experience with the sea. Captain Patterson, the first keeper, came to the Pacific Coast in 1823 on board the ship *Mentor.* James

Marner, keeper from 1888 to 1896, also spent many years at sea and, before his appointment as a lightkeeper, had worked on board the lighthouse tender *Manzanita.*

In 1872 the principal keeper earned $1,000 a year, paid quarterly. By the 1880s and '90s, however, the salary for that position had *decreased* to $800 a year. During this time, first assistants earned $600, second assistants $550, and third assistants $500 annually. "A very penny wise, pound foolish, policy of economy has been adopted by the government, by which the salaries of these men have been cut down to a mere pittance...," said one writer in 1883. "When it is considered how these men have to live, far removed from society, subject to the dangers and fatigues incident to their vocation, and the great responsibility which rests upon their shoulders, it would seem that the government could well afford to be far more liberal in remunerating their services. The fate and destiny of valuable property and precious lives are in their hands."[19] In spite of such criticisms, Congress did not appropriate funds for salary increases until well into the 1900s.

In the late 1800s, men had to meet several requirements to be appointed a lighthouse keeper. They had to be between the ages of eighteen and fifty; be able to read, write, and keep accurate accounts; be able to sail a boat; and have enough strength and mechanical ability to do the required manual labor, including making minor repairs about the premises. Nominations were made by the local Collector of Customs, who also had the title Superintendent of Lights. Despite attempts by the Lighthouse Board to eliminate politics from nominations, civil service reform was slow in coming. J. W. Patterson had officially served at the rank of keeper just two and one-half months before he was removed by the superintendent and replaced by Richard H. Fairchild. "The Government . . . can do about as it [has] a mind to with its servants," said the local newspaper, "but it seems hard that a gray-headed old man, who has spent his life in going down in ships and is

Richard H. Fairchild served as principal keeper from January, 1873, to October, 1875. (Courtesy U.S. Coast Guard)

now unprovided for, should be removed from a small office to subserve no other ends than those of politics."[20]

Pigeon Point originally had three keepers: a principal keeper plus a first and second assistant. In 1873 the position of third assistant was added. When the station was electrified in the 1920s, it was changed back to a three-man station, then again to a four-man station under the Coast Guard in the 1940s.

First and foremost among the keepers' duties was keeping the light burning brightly each night and the fog whistle operating during times of fog. The keeper on watch was required to remain in the watchroom and give continuous attention to the light while on duty. To do otherwise could cost the attending keeper his job. In September of 1895, for example, a keeper at the Point Arena light station was dismissed from the Lighthouse Service for just such a violation. As a warning to keepers at Pigeon Point and other lighthouses, Inspector Henry Nichols prepared a circular announcing the dismissal and required that it be posted at each station in his district.

The men lighted the oil lamp precisely at sunset so that it would reach maximum brightness as night came. The keepers worked regular shifts so that one keeper did not have to stay up all night and so that the work load would be divided equally. When the weather was calm, there was little to do besides wind up the clockwork every four hours or so and sit in the watchroom, perhaps reading a book by the glow of the lamp. During storms, the work got more exciting. The fog signal also required a keeper in attendance at all times during operation. To facilitate communication between keepers, especially in case of an emergency, electric call-bells were installed in 1880 between the tower, signal house, and dwelling.

Each morning, after extinguishing the lamp, the keeper would clean the equipment and fill the lamp with oil in preparation for relighting that evening. During the daytime, white linen curtains were hung in the lantern room to protect the lens from discoloration by sunlight.

The Lighthouse Board provided keepers with detailed, written instructions on operation of the station and with a thick book of regulations. Nothing was left to chance. Every detail of the operation of the equipment was spelled out, from how to trim a wick, to recipes for whitewash. Nightly, daily, weekly, and monthly duties were meticulously described.

The principal keeper had the added chore of keeping records. A list of forms kept at Pigeon Point light station in 1896 (and the number of copies of each) reveals the amount of paper work: vouchers for keeper's salaries (10), payroll forms (4), receipts for extra supplies (10), keeper's receipts for property on taking charge (2), annual property returns (4), returns of expenditures for oil, wicks, and chimneys (6), monthly reports of condition of station (36), fog signal reports (24), absence reports (18), and shipwreck reports (6). In addition, the keeper had to maintain record books that included a list of allowances for supplies; daily expenditures of oil, wicks, and chimneys; fog-signal records; a general account book; and a

Keepers ascended 136 iron steps each evening to light the lamp.
(Photo by the author)

daily journal of activities at the station noting the weather and any unusual events.

The lighthouse was open to visitors several days each week. A keeper dressed in his blue suit and cap would lead people up the spiral staircase to show them the giant lens and lamp. Some keepers enjoyed giving tours but would occasionally exaggerate their stories and explanations. In the fall of 1883 a reporter for the *San Mateo County Gazette* visited the station: "Our escort was of a very talkative disposition and took great pride in dilating upon the wonders of the establishment. As we stood inside the immense lens which surrounds the lamp, he startled us by stating in impressive tones that, were he to draw the curtains from the glass, the heat would be so great that the glass would melt instantly, and that human flesh would follow suit; we begged him not to experiment just then, and he kindly refrained."[21]

Many of the keepers had chosen the Lighthouse Service as their career and, after beginning as a second or third assistant, were eventually promoted to keeper. Often promotions came with transfers. Samuel M. Farran, appointed assistant keeper in January of 1873, was promoted the following year to keeper at East Brother light station on San Francisco Bay. In 1896 John McKenna was promoted to keeper at Pigeon Point after having served as first assistant at Point Reyes and then Point Sur.

For the most part, the keepers were hard working men who deserved the public's praise. In the government's register of keepers at Pigeon Point there is only one notation of removal due to "inefficiency," that in 1873. Some were genuine heroes such as John C. Ryan, who, in June of 1882, plunged into the surf near the lighthouse to rescue the little daughter of Manuel Silva. The girl was swept off the beach by a large wave and would surely have drowned had Ryan not swam to her rescue.

Though Pigeon Point was not isolated like the Farallones or St. George Reef, the keepers nevertheless lived in close quarters, and tempers sometimes flew. A letter to the inspector written in 1900 by Keeper McKenna accused First Assistant Louis Engilbrekt of using violent language at the station. The assistant vehemently denied the accusation, adding that he never spoke to the keeper except while on duty. Engilbrekt, in turn, accused McKenna of numerous improprieties including drunkenness while on duty and speaking abusively to Mrs. Engilbrekt. "I have not been in Pescadero since April 2nd," wrote the assistant in August. "At that time I asked him if I could go to town and he told me to go to Hell. After that I never asked to leave the station except to go fishing three times," he said. "I have been treated like a dog. . . ."[22] Both were veterans of the service, and it appears the inspector was uncertain whom to believe. Engilbrekt eventually resigned, and McKenna later transferred to Lime Point.

In the late 1800s Pigeon Point was not only the site of a lighthouse, but also the location of a small shipping center and whaling station. In the 1860s a boom and cable were rigged up to load lumber and crops onto ships. A 30-by-100-foot warehouse was also erected. About the same time the lighthouse was built, a wharf with a grain chute at the end was constructed about 300 feet from the lighthouse reservation. The region exported potatoes, butter, cheese, whale oil, lumber, shingles, and grain—mostly to San Francisco. For a time there was even a post office and school, but these later closed.

Portuguese shore whalers established a station at Pigeon Point in about 1862, and it continued operation until 1895. In 1871 the station supported seventeen whalers. After sighting a gray or humpback whale from the top of the cliffs, the men set out in small, single-masted sailboats equipped with exploding harpoons. After the whale was killed and hauled ashore, the blubber was sliced from the carcass and rendered in giant iron pots at the base of the cliffs just east of the lighthouse. The oil fetched thirty to fifty cents a gallon.

In a letter dated November 5, 1865, an anonymous Pigeon Point resident described the community:

Pigeon Point wharf, 1890s. (Courtesy National Maritime Museum)

Portuguese whaling boats and equipment in the cove just east of the lighthouse, 1890s. (Courtesy Edward Conant)

There are four Portuguese families, one California family, a company of seventeen Portuguese, a company of six wreckers, one Scotchman who superintends the landing, one Yankee and five children.

There are seven dwelling-houses here—all of the one-story description. They are nearly all new, and look very neat. Every house has a toilet attached, and arranged in the most elegant manner. . . . Beef, fish, potatoes and bread form our regular daily fare. The only way we get a change is by turning the bill-of-fare wrong end up, substituting bread, potatoes and fish first, and leaving beef to the last. Beans and salt are unknown in this region for table use. At each meal the doors are left wide open, and Old Neptune blows in salt enough to season each dish. The wind blows here daily a perfect hurricane—wilting the dignity of standing collars and stove-pipe hats.

Stove-pipe hats, biled shirts, store cloths, and civilization are but little known at Pigeon Point. But everybody is civil. The oldest inhabitant knows not of a fight ever having taken place here.[23]

The tranquility was marred in 1875, however, by the murder of wharfinger Alexander "Scotty" Rae. Mr. Rae managed the landing for the firm of Goodall, Nelson, and Perkins of San Francisco. While Rae was peacefully eating his breakfast on the morning of July 2, the telegraph operator ran to him shouting that the office had been seized by two men. Rae grabbed a large revolver and walked onto the wharf where three men, also armed, stood. Several shots were fired almost simultaneously according to Keeper Fairchild and his daughter, who later testified in court. Five bullets penetrated Rae, killing him within minutes. The men were employed by Loren Coburn, who claimed ownership of the landing. Coburn and four men were arrested and tried in Redwood City where witnesses testified that Rae had fired first. After the first trial ended in a hung jury, the case was retried and the five men found not guilty. Coburn wisely decided to settle in court the question of who owned the wharf and, a year later, won his case.

The lighthouse and fog signal nearly put an end to major shipwrecks at Pigeon Point, but not quite. On July 14, 1896, the Pacific Mail Steamship Company's liner *Colombia* ran aground a short distance south of the lighthouse. The five-year-old steamer was making her first run from Panama to San Francisco in what would have been record time. Though thick fog cut visibility to barely 100 feet, Captain William Clark continued at full throttle, hoping for fame. Instead he achieved disgrace.

Captain Clark heard a fog signal that he believed to be from Pigeon Point, though it must have been from Año Nuevo Island. He then heard a second signal (actually Pigeon Point) but said it sounded as though it came from several miles out at sea. Believing this signal was from an approaching vessel, Clark turned his ship slightly eastward to avoid a collision, and it was then that she struck the rocks. Clark reportedly had no idea where he was when he landed. Lighthouse authorities remained baffled as to how the captain could confuse two signals with such markedly different characteristics.

The event mostly generated amusement, except among the owners and captain. None of the passengers was hurt, and all remained on board for quite some time, at first believing that the vessel would be pulled free of the rocks. Old-time residents of the region were quick to recall the wrecks of the *Carrier Pigeon* and *Sir John Franklin* and the bounty cast up by the waves. Huge crowds flocked to Pigeon Point to view the doomed steamer. According to one observer, city folks had great fun "rescuing from the breakers the little yellow limes that swam shoreward to be salvaged. . . ."[24] From land, the ship gave the appearance of simply being anchored. Keeper James Marner was on watch when he heard the ship strike. "I thought it was the tender *Madroño* that had come up in the fog and dropped her anchor," he said. "I hollered to the boys, and they ran to put on

James Marner served eight years as principal keeper, resigning in 1896. (Courtesy Santa Cruz Public Library)

The *Colombia,* owned by the Pacific Mail Steamship Company, ran aground just south of Pigeon Point in 1896. The 327-foot-long steamer eventually broke up. (Courtesy San Mateo County Historical Museum)

Wreck of the Colombia. (Courtesy Ron Duarte)

their good clothes to receive the inspector, but we found our mistake. I could make out the *Colombia*. She was right up almost on dry land, and my fog horn blowing twice a minute all night. This is one of the queerest accidents I ever knew of, and I've been thirty-five years at sea."[25]

It soon became apparent that the ship could not be saved. "D'ya see how she fights for life?" said the gray-haired keeper from atop the lighthouse. "Ah, it's too bad. She won't let go of the rock. She's afraid of going down if she does. She thinks she'll hold on and live a little longer. But it's useless my boy. It's useless. She can't live. Over twenty-six feet of water in her forward compartment, a big rock sticking straight up in her bow and holding her there while the sea whips her tail and rolls her round like a piece of drift."[26] During the next few weeks, the owners retrieved much of the cargo and machinery, leaving the rest to the mercy of the sea or for others to salvage.

The vessel did not give in as easily as many people thought. A year later part of the hull still remained, and industrious nearby residents salvaged moldings from the state rooms, hundreds of feet of copper wire, and tons of white lead paint. Soon, every house in the area had copper clothes lines and a fresh coat of paint. It is said that one man earned enough from the wreck to purchase a home in Half Moon Bay.

Following pages: This remarkable view was taken after construction of the new fog signal building in 1899 but prior to the building of the addition to the north side of the dwelling in 1906. Note the large pile of cordwood to fuel the fog whistle. (Courtesy The Bancroft Library)

61

The *Cleone* takes on a load of lumber at Pigeon Point, about 1917. (Courtesy Edward Conant)

The Davis family of Pigeon Point, circa 1920. Frank Davis (second from left) with his parents (seated at right), brothers, and sisters. (Courtesy Frank E. Davis)

Later Years at the Lighthouse

The early 1900s brought many changes for Pigeon Point, both physical changes to the buildings and administrative changes within the Lighthouse Service. In 1910 the Lighthouse Board, which had administered the nation's lighthouse system since 1852, was replaced by the Bureau of Lighthouses. The bureau was under the Commerce Department and for most of its existence was headed by George Putnam, Commissioner of Lighthouses. The Lighthouse Service became strictly a civilian agency, from the commissioner right down to the district superintendents and keepers. Nevertheless, uniforms and strict discipline still came with the job.

This period of the station's history is within memory of several central California residents who grew up in or about the lighthouse. Frank E. Davis of Santa Clara was born at Pigeon Point in 1899 in a small farmhouse only a few hundred feet from the light station. His father, Joseph Davis, having spent the early part of his life as a ship's carpenter, immigrated to this country from the Azores. He settled at Pigeon Point around 1883 to raise a family and to farm the surrounding hillsides. The family leased land from Loren Coburn and grew grain, which was harvested once a year and shipped to Santa Cruz.

As a young man, Frank Davis knew many of the lightkeepers: John E. Lind, Carl E. Reit, Andrew L. Crandell, Isaac Knutsen, Lemuel C. Miner, Joseph A. Sylvia, and John Nixon to name a few. His sister, Mary, married First Assistant Miner in 1909. "Most of the men would stay four or five years," says

Keeper John E. Lind with his wife, circa 1910. Lind helped build St. George Reef lighthouse and later became keeper of the lighthouse at Crescent City. (Courtesy Frank E. Davis)

Davis, "then move on to another station."[27] In 1913 his brother-in-law was transferred to Cape Mendocino and later to Point Reyes and then to Yerba Buena Island, at that time popularly called "Goat Island."

Hauling the supplies delivered by lighthouse tender was always a huge job. Davis's father had the contract for the job at $2 per ton. The tender *Sequoia* would drop anchor a little way off shore, and the ship's crew would first haul the supplies to the beach by dory. "It then took four of us men with four horses most of the day to cart the forty tons of coal, kerosene, and other supplies from the beach to the lighthouse," recalls Davis.

During the 1906 earthquake the mighty brick tower survived virtually unscathed. Keeper Lind discovered but one small crack in the masonry about forty feet up—testimony to

Assistant Keeper Lemuel Miner with his wife, Mary, at Yerba Buena Island light station. (Courtesy Frank E. Davis)

both sound construction and a solid bedrock location. The quake also generated small cracks in the chimneys and plaster ceilings of the keepers' dwelling, but the damage was not serious. Frank Davis was not quite seven at the time, but he still remembers seeing the huge clouds of smoke billowing up from the north as San Francisco burned: "Us kids were really scared."

Another memorable event occurred in 1908 when Teddy Roosevelt's Great White Fleet steamed by early one morning, the giant warships passing in single file. It was also high tide, but young Davis had another explanation for the high water: "I was just a kid about nine years old at the time and boy was I full of baloney. I said, 'You know, that fleet is so big that it swoll the ocean up.'"

The point continued to be the site of shipwrecks, though none were of the magnitude of earlier decades. In August, 1913, the steam schooner *Point Arena*, veteran of the coastal lumber trade, attempted to moor at Pigeon Point landing to pick up a load of tanbark. The sea was quite rough that day, remembers Davis, and according to his recollections, one of the ropes used to tie the ship to a mooring buoy became tangled around the propeller. The ship, which could not be properly maneuvered, was soon dashed against the rocks. All hands made it safely to shore, but the 233-ton vessel quickly became a total loss. It broke in half and, recalls Davis, was later burned so that it would not be a hazard to navigation. Besides, he says, it just would not have looked good to have a wrecked ship in front of a lighthouse.

On April 18, 1911, the German power schooner *Triton* struck a drifting log thirteen miles out. The ship, bound for Jaluit in the Marshall Islands, quickly sank. The two German officers and nine Polynesian crewmen rowed toward shore all night, guided by the Pigeon Point light. As they neared shore, Joe Davis directed them to the landing. That morning the lightkeeper, much to his amazement, found two Germans and a

Wreck of the *Point Arena,* August, 1913. Part of the bow of this ship was uncovered by storm waves in 1983 and is exhibited at Año Nuevo State Reserve. (Courtesy Frank E. Davis)

Assistant Keeper Joseph Sylvia painted this picture of the station around 1912. (Courtesy Frank E. Davis)

group of South Seas natives on his doorstep.

Mrs. Jessie M. Davis of Redwood City called the lighthouse home during the 1920s. Her father, Jesse E. Mygrants, served as an assistant keeper at Pigeon Point from 1924 until 1941. Her vivid recollections help paint a detailed picture of lighthouse life at that time.

Before joining the Lighthouse Service, Jesse Mygrants owned and operated a bakery in Pennville, Indiana, until the flour dust in the air began to irritate his throat, forcing him to seek another line of work. His brother, Lloyd, had joined the Lighthouse Service and was stationed at Piedras Blancas light station out on the West Coast. Jesse successfully applied for a lightkeeping job and was assigned to Point Arguello light station in southern California. Uncertain whether this new career would work out, he waited two years before sending for his wife, Minnie, and two daughters.

In September, 1923, while Mygrants was stationed at Point Arguello, seven navy destroyers ran aground nearby in a dense fog. The bizarre accident was to become the navy's largest peacetime loss. Jesse Mygrants and the other two keepers were aroused the night of the disaster by shouts of distress from five of the sailors afloat in a small raft. The keepers hauled the men up the steep, rugged cliffs that night with only the light of a hand lantern. Inside the lighthouse, the bruised and exhausted sailors were made comfortable and given medical assistance while two of the keepers patrolled the coastline until dawn in search of more survivors. Mygrants and the others received commendations from the navy and the secretary of commerce for rendering assistance to the men.

Point Arguello lacked a nearby school for daughters Rosamond and Jessie, so Mygrants requested that he be transferred to a "school station." In October, 1924, the family moved to Pigeon Point. Jessie, then in the eighth grade, attended Gazos Creek School located a couple of miles south of the lighthouse.

Mygrants served as a second assistant and later a first assistant at Pigeon Point. Watch hours and work hours were divided equally among the four men with four hours watch followed by eight hours off. The schedule rotated each week, and Mrs. Davis recalls that her father sometimes had difficulty sleeping. The ground-shaking blasts from the fog signal did not help matters. Fortunately, the Mygrants family lived on the east side of the dwelling away from the signal house, and this muffled the sound slightly.

When her father had an early watch, Jessie Mygrants sometimes did her homework under the lighthouse light. "There was a small desk in the watchroom," she remembers, "and there my father would help me with my algebra."[28] It was a quiet, peaceful place to work, with only the sound of the clockwork ticking away as the giant lens rotated ever so slowly above their heads.

In addition to standing watch at night, the men did chores

Jesse and Minnie Mygrants at Pigeon Point, 1930s. (Courtesy Jessie Davis)

Jesse and Minnie Mygrants with daughter Rosamond (left) and friend, February, 1927. (Courtesy Jessie Davis)

Beach picnic at Pigeon Point. Left to right: Etta Jaehne; Alice, Herman, and Claude Jaehne; Jesse Mygrants; Gerard Jaehne; Mr. Van Zandt (carpenter); Minnie Mygrants; and Katy Marhoffer; about 1933. (Courtesy Jessie Davis)

about the station each morning from nine o'clock until noon. There was always work to keep them busy, including maintaining and checking the light and fog signal equipment, painting, or making minor repairs. Polishing the brasswork was an especially big chore. In addition to the brass around the lens and clockwork, there were also brass fittings in the signal house and brass kerosene lamps in the residences. When the inspector came once a month, he expected everything to be very neat and tidy all about the station, inside and out. According to Edward Conant, who lived just up the road, the place was so clean you could have just about eaten off the floor.

Jesse Mygrants had absolutely no fear of heights—a trait desirable in lighthouse keepers. Each evening before sunset, the salt spray had to be cleaned from the glass of the lantern room. Mr. Mygrants or one of the other keepers would cling to the small ladder which hung from the lantern room roof 100 feet above the ground and carefully wipe each pane. Whitewashing the outside of the tower could be even more precarious. The men would rig up a wooden platform suspended by ropes from the lower balcony. They began at the bottom, gradually hoisting themselves upward as they worked.

By the 1920s keepers were paid monthly, at a rate somewhat higher than in earlier years. "My father earned $90 per month as second assistant," remembers Mrs. Davis, "and $100 per month after he was promoted." In addition, each year he received a month's vacation time.

The station's giant Victorian-style dwelling was divided into four apartments. Jessie grew to know some of the other station residents quite well. Sometimes the children played cards together in the evenings on the Mygrants' kitchen table while mother made fudge. On several occasions they went on beach picnics together.

For most of the 1920s the principal keeper was John Nixon. He was replaced by Gerard Jaehne, who lived in the upper west apartment with his wife, Etta, and several children.

Other assistant keepers in the 1920s and '30s were Fred Zimmerman, H. A. Bernsten, John Hart, August Nelson, a Mr. Day, Thomas Henderson, and Joe Marhoffer.

One of the most frightening events in the lighthouse's history occurred in the spring of 1933. The keepers were using blow torches to remove old paint from the outside of the Victorian before repainting it. Mygrants noticed that one of the nails remained hot. He then put his ear to the side and could hear the crackling of flames inside the wall. Soon, smoke started pouring from the building, and fearing that the house might burn to the ground, the families began frantically unloading their possessions. A young man from the U.S. Coast and Geodetic Survey, Frank Fullaway, was boarding with the Mygrants family at the time. "He was always joking around," recalls Mrs. Davis, "and he did not believe me when I said the house was on fire. He soon discovered that I wasn't kidding." The smoke attracted the attention of some immigrant farm workers from the nearby fields, and they ran over to offer assistance. Mrs. Jaehne put them to work rescuing belongings. Apparently, there was some sort of lack of communication, says Mrs. Davis. "The workers carefully carried the non-breakable items like bedding down the stairs but threw breakable items like jars of jelly and canned fruit out the window."

The keepers battled the blaze as best they could while waiting for the fire truck to arrive from Redwood City. The fire truck took forty-five minutes to reach the lighthouse—record time for the narrow, winding road over the mountains. When the fire was finally extinguished, the damage (mostly confined to the east side of the building) was not as severe as had been feared. In fact, the damage from the water and chemicals proved to be worse than that from the flames. For awhile Jessie and her parents had to eat their meals in the laundry house. Soon, however, the Victorian was cleaned up enough so that they could move back. That summer a crew of eight to ten carpenters, plumbers, electricians, and painters

Jessie and Rosamond Mygrants pose in front of house with their mother, circa 1927. (Courtesy Jessie Davis)

arrived from the lighthouse district headquarters to make repairs. Mrs. Mygrants had the job of feeding the crew. She not only made them three meals a day but also baked bread, cakes, and pies.

Supplies were delivered monthly by lighthouse tender as in earlier years. Each family was alloted four tons of coal per year for household heating and cooking. In addition, the families could buy flour, sugar, and other food through the commissary. These were delivered by tender as well.

During Prohibition (1920 to 1933), San Mateo County's isolated coastline, vast sparsely populated mountainous areas, and proximity to San Francisco made it a center for West Coast rumrunners, bootleggers, and moonshiners. Tens of millions of dollars in contraband whiskey was hauled ashore annually by rumrunners working in remote shoreline coves under cover of darkness. "Rum ships" from Canada would anchor outside the three-mile limit, sometimes taking weeks to unload the cases of booze into smaller boats from shore.

Pigeon Point was an ideal location for rumrunning: it was isolated, had a derrick for hoisting the liquor from the beach, and was close to the highway. "They were a rough bunch of characters," according to Jessie Davis, "and were very vigilant. They could recognize any car that wasn't local." The lighthouse residents were powerless to try to stop the illicit activity, even though the rumrunners used the government's derrick. When planning a landing, the rumrunners always chose a moonlight night. They posted lookouts and threw a chain across the telephone wires to short-circuit the lines and prevent someone from calling the government agents. For many, the risks were profitable. A single shipment could be worth $10,000. Jessie's husband, George, was a banker in Pescadero at the time and remembers patrons making some rather large deposits of cash. It was a time when you did not ask questions.

One night while Assistant Keeper Mygrants was on watch,

The fire damage was being repaired when this 1933 photo was taken. Front row, left to right: Gotha Mygrants, Frank Fullaway, Jessie Mygrants, and unknown. Jaehne boys in background. (Courtesy Jessie Davis)

one of the rumrunners came to him and demanded a ride down the coast. The keeper protested, saying that he absolutely could not leave his watch. The rumrunner then pulled out a revolver, giving Mygrants no choice but to comply. He took the man eight miles down the coast in the family's Model T. Mygrants did not reveal the incident to his family until many years later for fear of worrying them.

On another occasion, Jessie, her sister, and two young men were returning from a dance they had attended in Santa Cruz when, just before reaching the lighthouse, the car was stopped by one of the rumrunners. Though he must have recognized the car, he demanded to know what they were up to. The young driver explained that he was simply returning the girls to the lighthouse where they lived. "Well go straight into the house," said the man to the girls sharply. "We were both really scared," says Mrs. Davis. "We went right to bed and soon heard the squeaking of the winch as the liquor was hoisted up with the government's derrick."

The rumrunners usually eluded the Prohibition agents, probably due in part to tip-offs from the inside. On a few occasions, however, their landings were foiled. In May, 1925, a 75-foot launch called the *Pilgrim* came to grief on the rocks near the point with a cargo of 175 whiskey cases and 100 barrels of beer. The crew had disappeared. Later that year a Coast Guard cutter patrolling off the point captured a fishing schooner with 329 cases of whiskey stashed in its hold.

There were no serious shipwrecks near Pigeon Point during Jesse Mygrants' service, but there were a number of small ones. In September, 1934, for example, the *Ohio No. 5*, an eighty-ton sardine boat out of Monterey, ran up on the rocks. Fortunately, all twelve crew members were saved, though some had to swim the 200 yards to shore.

Offshore from Pigeon Point it was a different matter. In 1929 the worst maritime disaster in the region's history

The keepers took good care of their Victorian home, as shown in this 1938 view. (Courtesy U.S. Coast Guard)

shocked central Californians and, indeed, the nation. The passenger liner *San Juan* was steaming north when it collided with the oil tanker *S.C.T. Dodd* at night in a dense fog. The tanker's bow rammed the liner in the side, punching a hole so large that, according to eyewitnesses, you could have driven a train through it. The veteran liner disappeared into the Pacific in just five minutes, giving little chance for the crew and passengers to find life jackets or lower the life boats. Eighty-seven people perished, only forty-two were rescued.

In 1939 the maintenance and operation of lighthouses and other aids to navigation in the United States were transferred to the Coast Guard. The era of the Lighthouse Service, a separate branch of government since George Washington's time, came to an abrupt end. Keepers could either continue as civilians and be employed by the Coast Guard or join the Coast Guard and be assigned an appropriate rank. Many of the older men, like Jesse Mygrants, choose to remain civilian keepers. Mygrants retired in 1941 after nearly twenty years in the service.

In the 1940s, around the time the radio beacon was installed, Pigeon Point once again became a four-man station. Lighthouse keeping was still a round-the-clock job. In the radio room, giant time pieces, which were synchronized with master clocks in Washington, D.C., controlled the radio signals. Emergency gasoline-powered generators were kept ready in case of a power failure. With these generators, the light, radio beacon, and diaphone could all be kept operational.

During the Coast Guard years, the station continued to be a home for young families. Life was a mixture of the old and the new. Some of the coastguardsmen kept vegetable gardens near the dwelling and enjoyed fishing off the rocks during off hours. They could catch perch and cabezon, or pry abalone off the rocks at low tide. "Some didn't like it here and asked for a transfer," said Seaman First Class Mel Braunagel while stationed there in 1958, "but it suits me fine. We're on duty six

This 1950s aerial photo shows the station's rainshed and water tanks in the upper left. (Courtesy U.S. Coast Guard)

hours and off eighteen. We've got our own private fishing area, and good living quarters. If you like it here and can do the job, they'll let you stay as long as you want."[29]

Although the living quarters satisfied Braunagel, Coast Guard officials decided that more modern accommodations were in order. In 1960 the large Victorian, though still sound, was demolished and replaced by four vernacular cottages. Those who had grown up around the lighthouse hated to see the old building go. There were attempts to persuade the Coast Guard to move the building onto nearby private land to preserve it, but these attempts failed. Instead, the building was bulldozed over the cliff.

In the mid-1960s the Coast Guard launched its Lighthouse Automation Program (LAMP), with which it hoped to automate by the mid-1980s the roughly 400 lighthouses under its jurisdiction. It was an economy move, an effort to free personnel from lighthouse duty, thus making them available for the many other jobs entrusted to the Coast Guard: boating safety, search and rescue, merchant marine safety, environmental protection, port safety, and maritime law enforcement. With the implementation of LAMP, Pigeon Point light station's future grew increasingly uncertain.

In California, smaller stations were automated first, but the abandoned lighthouses proved to be attractive to squatters and vandals. At many locations this problem was resolved by demolishing the old buildings and installing modern vandal-proof towers of steel and concrete. Following outcries from historic preservation groups, the Coast Guard began to search for alternative uses for the stations, such as leasing the buildings to other government agencies or local historical societies. In the early 1970s, as automation of Pigeon Point grew near, several organizations sought use of the buildings. The University of California at Santa Cruz, for example, expressed interest in establishing a marine laboratory there. None of these proposals was adopted, however.

In 1960 the Coast Guard demolished the original dwelling and replaced it with four cottages. (Courtesy Ron Duarte)

In 1972, a twenty-four-inch rotating aero-beacon was attached to the railing outside the lantern room, replacing the light inside the fresnel lens. In 1974 monitoring devices at the Coast Guard headquarters on Yerba Buena Island were linked to Pigeon Point's light, fog signal, and radio beacon, thus completing automation. One Coast Guard family remained as caretakers and to ward off vandals.

In the meantime, public interest in the history and preservation of the lighthouse grew. In ceremonies held at the lighthouse on September 18, 1976, the San Francisco Section of the American Society of Civil Engineers declared the lighthouse a California Historic Civil Engineering Landmark—at that time one of only sixteen such structures in the state to be so honored. Public access to the station, however, was limited to a few special occasions. When the Coast Guard offered tours of the station during three weekends in March, 1978, over 6,500 people showed up. This was certainly a far cry from the 10 or

12 Sunday afternoon visitors typical of the 1920s. Overwhelmed by the experience, the Coast Guard was understandably hesitant about doing *that* again.

On October 3, 1980, ceremonies were again held at the lighthouse as state park and Coast Guard officials joined to unveil a large brass plaque declaring the lighthouse a State Historic Landmark. The lighthouse was also placed on the National Register of Historic Places.

By this time, an alternative use had at last been found for those station buildings no longer needed by the Coast Guard. In 1980 the Coast Guard agreed to lease the land containing the dwellings and fog signal building to the State Department of Parks and Recreation. The state, in turn, agreed to sublease it to the American Youth Hostels, Inc., a private, non-profit organization that operates a nationwide chain of hostels patterned after European youth hostels. In late 1980 and early 1981

The lighthouse at dusk. (Photo by the author)

the four Coast Guard cottages were converted to low-cost, dormitory-style accommodations for overnight guests. In addition, the fog signal building was made into a meeting room both for hostel guests and other groups. The lighthouse has proven to be an ideal location for a hostel, attracting a diversity of users including many foreign visitors.

In 1984 the Año Nuevo Interpretive Association, with the cooperation of the Pigeon Point Hostel and the U.S. Coast Guard, established a program of regular public tours at the lighthouse. Volunteers not only conduct the tours but also help with upkeep of the facility including cleaning the lens and painting. Funds from tour fees are used to help purchase materials for lighthouse maintenance and restoration.

Through the years the Coast Guard's budget for lighthouse upkeep has been gradually cut. In the meantime, wind, rain, and salt air have continued to take their toll on the masonry and ironwork. Only through continued public interest and support can this and other lighthouses be appropriately preserved. Pigeon Point light station now serves more purposes than ever before, making continued preservation a particularly worthy goal. It is not only an aid to navigation, but also a link in a chain of coastal hostels and a landmark that preserves a small yet significant slice of maritime history.

Notes

1. U.S., Coast Survey, *Report of the Superintendent of the Coast Survey, showing the Progress of the Survey during the year 1854,* pp. 219-220.

2. U.S., Coast Survey, *Report of the Superintendent of the Coast Survey, showing the Progress of the Survey during the year 1855,* p. 406.

3. Albert S. Evans, *A La California: Sketches of Life in the Golden State* (San Francisco: G. W. Bancroft, 1889), p. 49.

4. "Wreck of the Sir John Franklin," *Santa Cruz Sentinel,* January 21, 1865, p. 2.

5. "A Few Particulars Concerning the Wreck of the Sir John Franklin," *San Mateo County Gazette,* February 11, 1865.

6. "Wreck of the British Bark 'Coya' at New Year's Point," *San Mateo County Gazette,* December 1, 1866.

7. Ibid.

8. "Loss of the 'Hellespont,'" *San Mateo County Gazette,* November 28, 1868.

9. "Let Us Have Light," *Daily Alta California,* November 30, 1868, p. 3.

10. "Pigeon Point Light-House," *San Mateo County Gazette,* June 10, 1871, p. 2.

11. "Memorandum for Mr. Molera," undated, manuscript collection, Society of California Pioneers Library, San Francisco.

12. Arnold Burges Johnson, *The Modern Light-House Service* (Washington, D.C.: Government Printing Office, 1890), p. 51.

13. "Our Coast Neighbors," *San Mateo Times and Gazette,* September 8, 1883, p. 2.

14. *Illustrated History of San Mateo County, California* (Oakland, California: Moore and DePue, 1878), p. 25.

15. George Putnam to Harry Rhodes, May 2, 1924. Letter in collection of Aids to Navigation Branch, Twelfth District, U.S. Coast Guard.

16. "San Gregorio Letter," *San Mateo County Gazette,* May 25, 1872, p. 2.

17. Ibid.

18. "Pescadero Letter," *San Mateo County Gazette,* September 23, 1871, p. 2.

19. *History of San Mateo County, California* (San Francisco: B. F. Alley, 1883), p. 222.

20. *San Mateo County Gazette,* February 15, 1873, p. 1.

21. "Our Coast Neighbors," *San Mateo Times and Gazette,* September 8, 1883, p. 2.

22. Louis Engilbrekt to U. Sebree, August 9, 1900. Copy of letter in collection of Aids to Navigation Branch, Twelfth District, U.S. Coast Guard.

23. "Letter From Pigeon Point—Santa Cruz Co.," *Pajaro Valley Times,* November 11, 1865, p. 2.

24. "The Colombia Can Not Be Saved," *San Francisco Examiner,* July 16, 1896.

25. "On the Rocks in a Dense Fog," *San Francisco Examiner,* July 15, 1896.

26. *San Francisco Examiner,* July 16, 1896.

27. Interview with Frank E. Davis, February 23, 1981 and June 21, 1986. All of the quotations by Mr. Davis are from these interviews with the author.

28. Interview with George and Jessie Davis, April 8, 1986 and June 10, 1986. All of the quotations by Mrs. Davis are from these interviews with the author.

29. Wally Trabing, "Behind-The-Scenes Story of Lighthouse," *Santa Cruz Sentinel,* July 27, 1958, p. 10.

Further Reading

Gibbs, James A. *Lighthouses of the Pacific*. West Chester, Penn.: Shiffer Publishing Ltd., 1986.

———. *West Coast Lighthouses*. Seattle: Superior Publishing Co., 1974.

Holland, Francis Ross., Jr. *America's Lighthouses: Their Illustrated History Since 1716.* Brattleboro, Vermont: The Stephen Greene Press, 1972.

Hynding, Alan. *From Frontier to Suburb: The Story of the San Mateo Peninsula*. Belmont, Calif.: Star Publishing Co., 1982.

Le Boeuf, Burney J., and Kaza, Stephanie, eds. *The Natural History of Año Nuevo*. Pacific Grove, Calif.: The Boxwood Press, 1981.

Morrall, June. *Half Moon Bay Memories*. El Granada, Calif.: Moonbeam Press, 1978.

Perry, Frank. *East Brother: History of an Island Light Station*. Point Richmond, Calif.: East Brother Light Station, Inc., 1984.

———. *Lighthouse Point: Reflections on Monterey Bay History*. Soquel, Calif.: GBH Publishing, 1982.

Shanks, Ralph C., Jr., and Shanks, Janetta Thompson. *Lighthouses and Lifeboats on the Redwood Coast*. San Anselmo, Calif.: Costaño Books, 1978.

Shanks, Ralph C., Jr., and Shanks, Janetta Thompson. *Lighthouses of San Francisco Bay*. San Anselmo, Calif.: Costaño Books, 1978.

Stanger, Frank M. *South From San Francisco: The Life Story of San Mateo County*. San Mateo, Calif.: San Mateo County Historical Association, 1963.

Typesetting: Typola
Printing: Community Printers
Santa Cruz, California